MW01174102

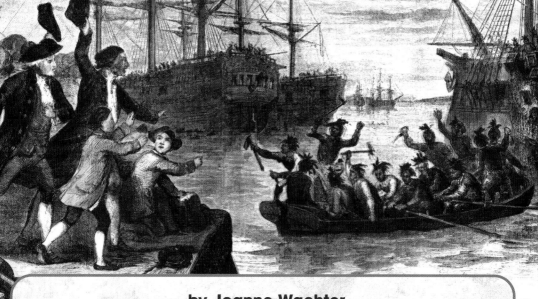

**by Joanne Wachter**

## Table of Contents

Introduction . . . . . . . . . . . . . . . . . . . . . . . . . . . . . . . . 2

**Chapter 1** Why Did the Boston Tea Party Happen? . . 4

**Chapter 2** What Happened at the
Boston Tea Party? . . . . . . . . . . . . . . . . . . . . . . 8

**Chapter 3** What Happened After the
Boston Tea Party? . . . . . . . . . . . . . . . . . . . . . 12

**Chapter 4** What Happened After
the British Made More Laws? . . . . . . . . . . . 16

Summary . . . . . . . . . . . . . . . . . . . . . . . . . . . . . . . 20

Glossary . . . . . . . . . . . . . . . . . . . . . . . . . . . . . . . 22

Index . . . . . . . . . . . . . . . . . . . . . . . . . . . . . . . . . 24

# Introduction

The year was 1773. There were thirteen British **colonies** in North America. The people in the colonies were **colonists**.

Lake Superior

Lake Michigan

Lake Huron

Lake Ontario

Lake Erie

North America

New Hampshire

Maine
(part of Massachusetts)

Massachusetts

New York

Rhode Island

Connecticut

Pennsylvania — New Jersey

— Delaware

Virginia — Maryland

North Carolina

Atlantic Ocean

South Carolina

Georgia

There were thirteen British colonies.

Scotland

England

Wales

## Did You Know?

British means belonging to Great Britain.

Some colonists were angry at **Great Britain**. These colonists were **Patriots**. Read to find out what the Patriots did. Read about the **Boston Tea Party**.

▲ Some colonists were angry.

# Words to Know

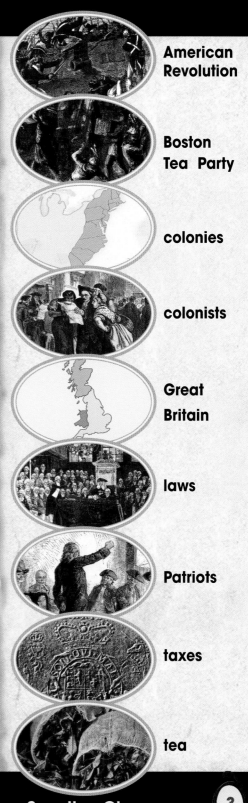

American Revolution

Boston Tea Party

colonies

colonists

Great Britain

laws

Patriots

taxes

tea

See the Glossary on page 22.

# Why Did the Boston Tea Party Happen?

The colonists had to pay British **taxes**. The colonists had to pay British taxes on newspapers.

Colonists had ▲ to pay taxes on newspapers.

▲ This is a British tax stamp.

The colonists had to pay taxes on **tea**.
Some colonists were angry about the taxes.

▲ Colonists had to pay taxes on tea.

The angry colonists were Patriots. The Patriots did not want British tea. The Patriots did not want to pay British taxes.

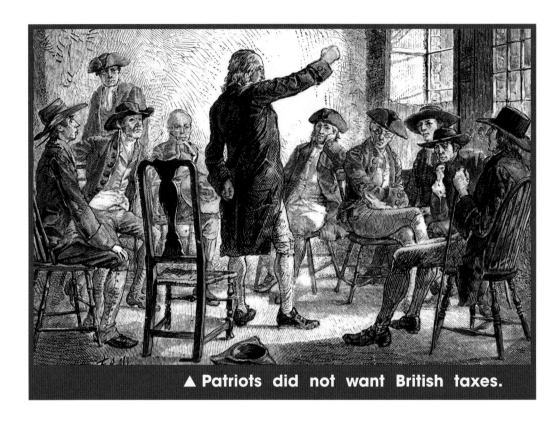

▲ Patriots did not want British taxes.

## People to Know

Paul Revere and John Hancock were Patriots.

▲ Paul Revere

▲ John Hancock

The Patriots were angry. The Patriots wanted to do something about tea. They wanted to do something about taxes.

▲ Patriots did not want to pay taxes.

## Learn More

Read these books about the Patriots.
Jean Fritz wrote the books.
*Why Don't You Get a Horse, Sam Adams?*
*And Then What Happened, Paul Revere?*
*Will You Sign Here, John Hancock?*

# What Happened at the Boston Tea Party?

It was a December night in 1773. Men climbed onto three British ships.

▲ Ships brought tea to Boston Harbor.

The British ships were in Boston Harbor. The ships carried boxes of tea. The ships carried 342 boxes of tea leaves.

▲ Tea is made from tea leaves.

Patriots climbed onto the ships. The Patriots were dressed as Native Americans. The Patriots opened the boxes of tea.

▲ The Patriots opened the boxes of tea.

The Patriots threw British tea in the water. This was the Boston Tea Party.

## It's a Fact

The Boston Tea Party helped start the American Revolution.

## People to Know

Samuel Adams was leader of the Patriots.

▲ Samuel Adams

11

# What Happened After the Boston Tea Party?

The Boston Tea Party made Great Britain angry. The British leaders were very angry. The British king was very angry.

## Solve This

George III became king in 1760. George III was king until 1820. How many years was George III the king?

Answer: 60 years

▲ George III was king of Great Britain.

The British leaders made new **laws**. The laws were about the Boston Tea Party.

▲ The British leaders made laws.

Boston Harbor was closed. No ships could go in or out. The colonists had to pay for the tea. Then the harbor could open.

The laws made the Patriots angry.

▲ Boston Harbor was closed.

The British leaders made more laws. Colonists could not have meetings. Colonists had to feed British soldiers.

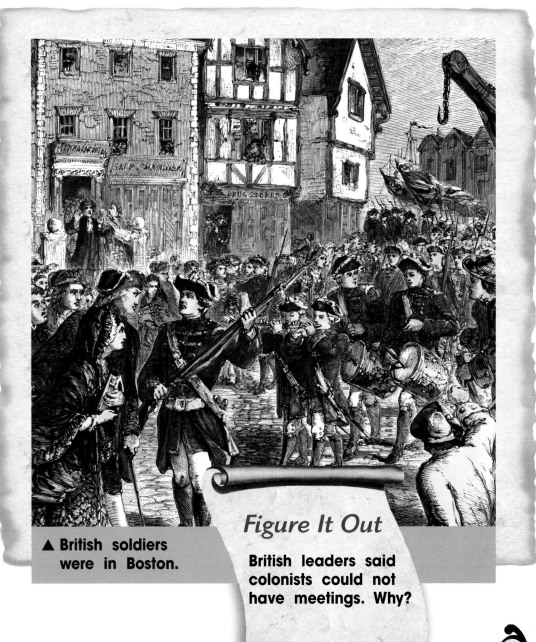

▲ British soldiers were in Boston.

*Figure It Out*

British leaders said colonists could not have meetings. Why?

# What Happened After the British Made More Laws?

Patriots did not like British laws. Patriots in all the colonies were angry.

Patriots from all the colonies had a meeting. They talked about British laws. The Patriots decided what to do.

▲ Patriots talked about the British laws.

The Patriots did not trade with Great Britain. The Patriots trained soldiers. Some Patriots were soldiers.

▲ Patriots were soldiers.

Soon, the colonies fought with Great Britain. The **American Revolution** began.

▲ The Patriots fought with Great Britain.

**Then & Now**  The American Revolution was a war with Great Britain. Now America and Great Britain are friends.

# Summary

Patriots were angry at Great Britain. Some Patriots had the Boston Tea Party. The Boston Tea Party helped start the American Revolution.

| | **Why Did the Boston Tea Party Happen?** |
|---|---|
| Colonists had to pay taxes on newspapers. | |
| Colonists paid taxes on British tea. | |
| Patriots did not want British tea. | |
| Patriots did not want to pay taxes. | |
| Patriots had the Boston Tea Party. | |

## The Boston Tea Party

| | **What Happened at the Boston Tea Party?** |
|---|---|
| Men climbed onto three British ships. | |
| The Patriots opened the boxes of tea. | |
| The Patriots threw British tea in the water. | |

| **What Happened After the Boston Tea Party?** | Great Britain was angry. |
| --- | --- |
| | Great Britain made new laws. |
| | Great Britain closed Boston Harbor. |
| | Colonists could not have meetings. |
| | Colonists had to feed soldiers. |

| **What Happened After the British Made More Laws?** | British laws made Patriots angry. |
| --- | --- |
| | Patriots helped Massachusetts. |
| | Patriots would not trade with Great Britain. |
| | Patriots trained soldiers. |
| | The American Revolution began. |

## Think About It

1. What was the Boston Tea Party?
2. Why did the Boston Tea Party happen?
3. The Boston Tea Party helped start the American Revolution. How?

**American Revolution** a war between the thirteen colonies and Great Britain

*Patriots fought in the American Revolution.*

**Boston Tea Party** the time when Patriots threw British tea in the water

*Patriots had the Boston Tea Party.*

**colonies** places owned by a country

*North America had thirteen colonies.*

**colonists** people who lived in the colonies

*Some colonists lived in Massachusetts.*

Scotland

England

Wales

**Great Britain** the countries of England, Scotland, and Wales

*England was part of Great Britain.*

**laws** rules

*British leaders made new laws.*

**Patriots** colonists who were angry at Great Britain

*Patriots did not like British laws.*

**taxes** money paid to the government

*Patriots did not want taxes.*

**tea** dried leaves used to make a drink

*Patriots threw British tea in the water.*

# Index

Adams, Samuel, 11

American Revolution, 11, 19–20

Boston Harbor, 9, 14

Boston Tea Party, 3, 11–13, 20

colonies, 2, 16–17, 19

colonists, 2–6, 14–15

Great Britain, 2–3, 12, 18–20

Hancock, John, 6

King George III, 12

laws, 13–17

Native Americans, 10

North America, 2

Patriots, 3, 6–7, 10–11, 14, 16–18

Revere, Paul, 6

soldiers, 15, 18

taxes, 4–7

tea, 5–7, 9–11, 14, 20